DEREK WALCOTT

O STARRY STARRY NIGHT

Derek Walcott was born in St. Lucia in 1930. He is the author of fourteen colle[...] poetry, numerous plays, and a book of essays. [...] bel Prize in Literature in 1992.

O STARRY

STARRY NIGHT

A PLAY

DEREK WALCOTT

FARRAR, STRAUS AND GIROUX

NEW YORK

Farrar, Straus and Giroux
18 West 18th Street, New York 10011

Library of Congress Cataloging-in-Publication Data
Walcott, Derek.
O starry starry night : a play / Derek Walcott.
    pages   cm
    ISBN 978-0-374-22707-4
    1. Gogh, Vincent van, 1853–1890—Drama.   2. Gauguin, Paul, 1848–1903—
Drama.   3. Painters—Europe—Drama.   I. Title.

PR9272.9.W3 O33 2014
812'.54—dc23
                                                                2013033164

Designed by Abby Kagan

Farrar, Straus and Giroux books may be purchased for educational, business, or
promotional use. For information on bulk purchases, please contact the Macmillan
Corporate and Premium Sales Department at 1-800-221-7945, extension 5442,
or write to specialmarkets@macmillan.com.

www.fsgbooks.com
www.twitter.com/fsgbooks • www.facebook.com/fsgbooks

P1

TO MY SON, PETER,

AND

TO SIGRID

O STARRY STARRY NIGHT

O Starry Starry Night premiered at the Lakeside Theatre at the University of Essex on May 2, 2013, with the following cast:

VINCENT VAN GOGH	Brian Carter-Green
PAUL GAUGUIN	Wendell Manwarren
THEO VAN GOGH	Nigel Scott
LOTTE	Martina Laird
CAFÉ PROPRIETOR	David Tarkenter
ZOUAVE SOLDIER	Michael Prokopiou
CAFE MUSICIAN	Julian Harries

Directed by Derek Walcott and Barbara Peirson.
Lotte's song composed by Galt McDermott.
Van Gogh and Gauguin paintings on stage by Peter Walcott and Gary Butte.

For its Caribbean premieres in St. Lucia and Trinidad, the role of Lotte was played by Natalie LaPorte; in Trinidad the musician was played by Gene Lawrence.

CAST OF CHARACTERS

CAFÉ PROPRIETOR, JOSEPH GINOUX, *age 60*

PAUL GAUGUIN, *a painter, age 40*

LOTTE, *a prostitute, age 35*

VINCENT VAN GOGH, *a painter, age 35*

THEO VAN GOGH, *his brother, an art dealer, age 31*

YOUNG ROULIN, *a Zouave, a young soldier, age 25*

The action takes place in Arles, in the south of France, in 1888.

Prologue

[VINCENT *appears on a hilltop overlooking Arles;*
stars, street ablaze below him.]

VINCENT

O starry, starry night, how shall I exult?
Your fruit hangs heavily in the branched sky,
your floor is scattered with the fallen crystals
of remembered constellations, your wild orbs plummet,
your fountains all jet reverential praise
your tears are the gliding sorrow of some behemoth,
like a thousand pharoses on the dark sea;
processional pilgrims and sentinels
over our streets and cities, steer us home.
Home, home towards heaven. O starry, starry night!

[*A distant train, coming nearer. Fade. A starry sky.*]

[*The café. Arles. Two pieces of luggage flying into the street.*
LOTTE *appears, raging.*]

LOTTE

Let me tell you something, Monsieur Ginoux!
I have been thrown out of better establishments
than this fleas' nest, this cockroach circus,
you, you, you, you, you, you louse's mother's man!
You'll know better than messing with an
Algerian woman. I know you, you'll take me back,

5

because this dump requires my devotion.
Don't mess with Lotte or she'll cut your turkey-wattled
throat while you're asleep. Not that she'd sleep with you!
I'd rather sell chestnuts on the streets of Paris
than work in this bloody backwater Arles!
You deputy assistant to the deputy mayor, you!

ACT I

Scene One

[Pre-dawn in Arles. A café pavement, under an awning.
GAUGUIN *sits at a table, drinking a coffee. Lamps fading.*
The PROPRIETOR, *sweeping, pauses, points.]*

PROPRIETOR

Now dawn will set those cypresses on fire.
If you stay here, you'll see the miracle.
Our city's not a city but a fair-sized town;
it's famous for a dent in its Roman wall
that bears, if you look very hard, the imprint
of Christ's knee. I know it's a long way
from Jerusalem, but I believe it.
I believe it's capable of breeding saints
in spite of its brothels. There're five.
Brothels, not saints.
Look, the fog is sneaking out of the city streets
like a thief, leaving our avenue bare
and stripped of everything but the sun. Coffee?

*[*GAUGUIN *shakes his head no, then covers*
his cup with one palm.]

I've managed this place for centuries.
I know it like my hand. Arles is nice.
Your friend the Dutchman lives in the yellow house,
but you don't want to wake him. I understand.
Three, wait, let me see, three corners up.

9

[LOTTE *enters with an umbrella, stands behind a garbage bin.*
Begins to undress, half hidden. GAUGUIN *watches.*]

LOTTE

The sky's bladder is as full as mine.
It's going to rain.

[*She stoops behind the bin.*]

GAUGUIN

Madam, pardon.

LOTTE

Did you just get off the train?

GAUGUIN
[*Nods.*]

LOTTE

From Paris?

GAUGUIN
[*Lifts eyebrow, nods.*]

LOTTE

Boy, you're really talkative, aren't you?
What do you plan to do
in this shithole of a town?

GAUGUIN
[Removes pipe, gestures with it.]
Paint.

LOTTE
Paint? There's nothing to paint here.
I'm from here. There's nothing.
Just in case you ask. I'm a . . .
Well, you can judge for yourself.
My name's Lotte.

GAUGUIN
Good morning, Lotte.
But are you doing what I think you are?

LOTTE
Having a municipal pee. Yes.

GAUGUIN
Madame,
would you prefer to use the facility
of that yellow house across the street?

LOTTE
[Crouching behind the garbage bin.]
Hold on. I'll soon be finished. Good.
How about you? Would you care to share

the facility behind this box with me?
Or over in those bushes there? Fifty francs.

[*She rises, straightens her dress.*]

GAUGUIN

Some other time. Everything is yellow here, or gold.
The yellow sunrise in the cornfields.
A prostitute's pee, and that gangrenous
yellow house.

[*Crosses the street, shouts.*]

Vincent! He's here! The wild bull
from the pampas of Peru! Gauguin is here!

LOTTE
[*Shouts.*]
I'll see you around. *Bonjour*, Monsieur Gauguin.

[*Turns, goes up the street, steps carefully over
something on the sidewalk, exits.*]

VINCENT's *voice*
Come in! Come in! The door is open, Paul.
I'm making breakfast. The sausages are burning.

[GAUGUIN *heads towards the yellow house
with his luggage.*]

GAUGUIN

I don't want breakfast. I want to sleep.
For six fucking months if possible.

[*He enters the yellow house.*]

[*Fade.*]

Scene Two

[VINCENT *and* GAUGUIN *in the kitchen,*
a cash box between them.]

GAUGUIN

Now, in this little box we put our capital, agreed?

VINCENT

Agreed. And I prefer that you keep it.

GAUGUIN

Okay. This is the arrangement with your brother:
Theo supports me at the rate of
two thousand francs a month, for which I send him
every canvas that I like and finish,
which he then sells to Goupil's at a cut.

VINCENT

The same with me.

GAUGUIN

Hold on. In exchange,
he's billed for all of my expenses.

VINCENT

Our expenses.

GAUGUIN

Food, drinks, paints, women.

VINCENT

Agreed. We're doing that.

GAUGUIN

What we are not doing is not accepting this:
that I shall be living in Arles forever,
that this agreement, as pleasant and as hospitable as it is,
    is not for good.

VINCENT

We'll see.

GAUGUIN

No, we will not see. You understand?

VINCENT

Yes! Now, you asked me about this painting.
I'll tell you how it happened.
I first beheld them, the family of Millet,

with their lantern-red, crooked Dutch faces,
ravaging their potatoes. One of them was Lotte,
delicate devourer of their only crop. I sat
away from them so I could see them better,
particularly Lotte. Her long, rabid fingers
moved as delicately as a queen's. The others
looked as if they had been hewn
from the mud of the Borinage.
They chewed with the voracity of machines.
I watched without the compassion of the evangelist
I was supposed to be; they were subjects,
and mentally I was drawing them.
My heart was riven by Lotte's bulging eyes,
by her false-flashing smile to me.
Reverend van Gogh like the lantern's wick,
raging with blasphemous lust.

GAUGUIN
[*An explosive laugh.*]
So they couldn't see what the minister
was hiding in his holy trousers?
Erect with the beatitude "Blessed are the poor"?
There's an eroticism to poverty.
How often have I admonished little Gauguin,
the scoundrel in my trousers, to behave!
But, Vincent, you preached and you believed, though?

LOTTE

[*In his hallucination.*]

God is consistent, Pastor. Every night
He gives us the same shit to eat.

VINCENT

Please sit down. I beg you. Sit down, girl.
So that, at least, your turmoil can settle.
Look through the windows at these thin poplars,
so skeletal in the snow. Turn, look.

GAUGUIN

Did they listen? Did *you* believe your sermon?

VINCENT

And look at the stars guttering like candles
above them. The poplars do not break;
the constellations keep their design
through the most blinding blizzard.
We are insignificant, a mouse in a coal mine,
scratching. Poplar to candle, mouse.

[*To* GAUGUIN.]

I didn't understand what I was saying,
but I was passionate and Lotte was radiant.

GAUGUIN

That's what belief is—doubt made consistent.

VINCENT

It was a word from Dante. "The Borinage."
Like the Malebolge. And, Paul, it was Inferno.
An absolute Inferno. Menu, boiled potatoes.
Lotte loosened her bodice strings a little
to let me feast on a white flash of flesh.

GAUGUIN

[*Rises.*]

A prelude to the whorehouse we're going to.
O white thighs in their black mesh! Vive Lautrec!

[*Offenbach music. Cancan as the lights fade and change.*]

Scene Three

[*Outside. A small hill overlooking the town of Arles.
A starry night with a full moon over shining roofs.
VINCENT and GAUGUIN descend the narrow road.
GAUGUIN stops after a few steps.*]

GAUGUIN

Stop. Monsieur van Gogh. Will you join me
in a tribute to your beloved little city Arles?
Pause and deliver!

[GAUGUIN *turns his back, unbuttons, begins to pee.*]

VINCENT

I shall join you in our golden tribute,
Monsieur Gauguin.

[*He also turns, unbuttons.*]

GAUGUIN
[*Sings.*]
Ach, du lieber Augustin, alles ist weg, weg.

VINCENT

That is German. Not French. Who the fuck
was Augustin?
[*Translating.*]
All is lost, lost, Augustin, but take it easy.
All is not, not lost.

GAUGUIN

The only thing that is lost
is a cascade of golden urine
from the second-greatest pisser in the world. ·

VINCENT

Who's first? Augustin?

GAUGUIN

Moi! Gauguin.
Your ancestors, the Romans, would have been

furious with you. Was it for this they built
their aqueduct? For your pathetic little pump?

VINCENT

I have ambition stronger than any aqueduct.
Look up, Monsieur Gauguin. I see those meteors
you humble pissers call the stars, like wheels
of perpetual motion, the primum mobile,
cartwheeling across the crouching roofs of Arles.
Someone has caught the candles of the sky
                    [*Hugs* GAUGUIN *around the neck.*]
to guide us home, my vagabond Breton.

GAUGUIN

Not home, not yet. It's too early, Reverend.

[*Silence.*]

VINCENT

I cannot tell you how happy I am
to have you here with me, how blest I am;
for the smell of the pines in the night, the rustle
in the comforting cypress, the tormented olives
who understand our suffering like our Lord's.

GAUGUIN

Your Lord, not mine.

VINCENT

He's ours, Gauguin.
He takes care of us. His corn-haired angels
stand guard over our yellow house. You'll see.
I have a lot of active passersby
to keep the canvases busy, but even the trees
are hectic in the wind; there's a lot of wind.
It sends the canvases flying off the easel.
Between the wind and the rooks, I tell you,
I look like a scarecrow, but that's not enough.

GAUGUIN

So shoot the fucking birds then! *Patow! Pow!*

[*Mimes firing a shotgun.*]

VINCENT

Great! We'll cook the rooks, cook the rooks! Okay.

[*They enter the café.*]

GAUGUIN

God, you're a talker, Vincent!

VINCENT

The government, we should talk about that.
See it! The best artists we respect, unite
in an aesthetic republic, one with light.

GAUGUIN

And women.

VINCENT

And women, too, of course.
Away from the pernicious, vampiric galleries,
the shouts of prices in the market,
under the benign rule of our government.

GAUGUIN

In a new landscape, one without churches,
brick barracks, near a blue ocean
and white reefs, I know just where.
For a new school of painting, an academy
built in the open, and the world's centre
will shift from Paris to the tropics.
From Montmartre to Martinique.

VINCENT

Cousin, we share one dream.
We'll sign it with red paint for blood.

GAUGUIN

To a new art. A different life! *Salud!*

VINCENT

I'll drink it in turpentine, the toast. *Santé!*

[*Drinks from the turpentine container.*]

Scene Four

[*Interior. The café.* L O T T E *singing to an accordion.*
V I N C E N T *and* G A U G U I N *enter.*]

LOTTE

Sad as the smoke of trains
from the small country station,
as the bright streets of Paris after it rains,
as my heart's resignation
that you have left me for good,
like the smoke that leaves from a hazy wood
in autumn. I should be sadder, I should
put you out of my mind, but we grow resigned
to arrivals and departures,
so, yes, I am resigned.

[V I N C E N T *and* G A U G U I N *applaud.*]

Scene Five

[*In the yellow house.* L O T T E *is looking at a Martinique painting.*]

GAUGUIN

This is Martinique. I lived there once.

LOTTE

Yes? What is Martinique like?

GAUGUIN

What is Martinique like?

Have you read Baudelaire? Charles Baudelaire? *Non.*

Well, it is like the happier verses of Baudelaire come true.

I can close my eyes now and see its blue horizons

humming with promise, all day

the volcano of Saint-Pierre smoking its pipe

like a contented peasant. I can see

the white thread of its waterfalls. I hear

the raucous racket of its parrots heading home

in the green dusk, *awkraaaaak.*

LOTTE

[*Laughs.*]

And the women there went naked?

GAUGUIN

Oh, no, they covered themselves, their breasts,

like pious Catholics. Like you.

LOTTE

Unless I pose for you, perhaps.

GAUGUIN

Perhaps.

Except I cannot promise to pay you.

LOTTE

I can wait to be paid. Shall I start?

[Begins to undress.]

GAUGUIN

On credit? Let's wait a little while. We'll see.
[Pause.]
Yes, all right. Go ahead, show me.

LOTTE
For free?

GAUGUIN

On credit.
[Laughs.]
Forget it. Another time perhaps.

[LOTTE *turns, bares her breasts.*]

LOTTE

What do you think?

GAUGUIN
Seriously. Another time.
They are beautiful.

LOTTE
[Covering up.]
Until age breaks them down.
All beauties become hags in the end.

GAUGUIN

Here—until that day.

[GAUGUIN *gives her money from his pockets.*]

LOTTE

You are most gracious, sir. A *chevalier.*

GAUGUIN

I am part of the Peruvian nobility
fallen on reprehensible times.
I recognize in you a lady of quality.

LOTTE

[*Curtseying.*]
Merci. Tell me some more.

GAUGUIN

Like what?

LOTTE

Are there many wild beasts there?

GAUGUIN

Oh, yes! I've never shot any, though.

LOTTE

What do they look like?

GAUGUIN

Like me.

Exactly like me. Two legs, two hands, a cock,
everything. They eat everything.
And they cannot be trusted. *Homo lupus.*
Man is a wolf. No; monkeys, snakes, some deer.

LOTTE

I love music and the theatre.

GAUGUIN

Then it is not for you, dear.

[VINCENT *enters, looks in, says nothing. Exits.*]

LOTTE

Who is that?

GAUGUIN

My landlord, Vincent.

LOTTE

I know. He comes to the café a lot.
The girls are all afraid of him.

GAUGUIN

Vincent? Nooooh. He's a dove, Vincent. Harmless.
But a very, very powerful painter.

[VINCENT *emerges, looks in, nods, then exits again.*]

LOTTE

He obviously wants me to go. I'm off.
Bring him with you to the café, to hear me.

GAUGUIN

We know you sing.

LOTTE

Like a frog. But they pay me.

[*Leaving,* LOTTE *encounters* VINCENT *at the door.*
He stares at her. She shudders, then leaves quickly.]

Scene Six

[*The studio.* VINCENT *and* GAUGUIN *at separate*
easels, side by side, but both painting landscape
with the cathedral.]

GAUGUIN

Forget the metaphysics, Van Gogh. Paint!
You are painting so that a wall,
a gate, could take a day, a week, a month
to get it right in the sunlight, or in shadow.
In that we're only artisans, not seers or prophets,
or metaphysicians or astronomers, but workmen

without visionary pretensions, like stonemasons.
We pave with paint—that's it!

VINCENT

That's not only it.

At least not for me.

GAUGUIN

And that's the problem.
There's nothing beyond our work. Just death.

[GAUGUIN *groans loudly, throws down his rag.*]

VINCENT

Why are you groaning? Paul! You're groaning.

GAUGUIN

The church, as usual, overlooking all.
Like a death's head, staring at me with empty eyes.
In Arles, in any autumn, just pick
an arbitrary September, it doesn't matter,
not as far as that cathedral is concerned.
We're all sinners, down to the guiltiest fly
washing its hands at the font; like me
or a painter cleaning his brushes.
One day I shall find it, the hedonist's paradise.
It was almost there in emerald Martinique
and its sapphire sea, except for its women,

whose breasts were covered; maybe the Marquesas,
if the missionaries haven't corrupted it
with chastity.

VINCENT

So move your easel.

GAUGUIN

I dream of a culture without any religion.
We'd be its saints: Saint Vincent and Saint Paul
in the new heterodoxy—if that's a word.

VINCENT

Then leave it out then.

GAUGUIN

Leave what out?

VINCENT

Out of the painting as out of your life—the church.

GAUGUIN

I can't do that. It would ruin the composition.
Or there'd be no composition.

VINCENT

As in art, so in life.

GAUGUIN

For you, Corporal, not for me.

[*Shouts towards the church.*]

Damn you!

[VINCENT *laughs.*]

VINCENT

You have to learn something. Here, in Arles,
days scud by over the roofs and lanes,
racing without an anchor. As for me,
my war is with the weather. In autumn, in Arles
the slates darken in the drizzle, the trees
thresh and toss, then the rain comes. I go out anyway,
my easel rifled on one shoulder anyway.
I have made my peace with the treacherous Midi.

GAUGUIN

You lied like a travel agent. Like a postcard.
You made everything so glorious.

[VINCENT *laughs.*]

God! What a miserable day.
We'll both stay home and paint the furniture.

VINCENT

Before you came, when I still lived alone,
I went down to Sainte-Marie to paint some boats.

I was so happy I thought I was insane.

That you would come out and paint with me at last,

not physical madness, but something closer

to the contorted ecstasy of the olives.

I felt the way you talk about Martinique:

the sea was tropical, cerulean shot with emerald,

and flecked with little mutinous white crests.

I stood thère, Paul, rooted and racked with joy,

with gratitude at what life offers us

in the short time we are given. It was bliss.

Bliss that ran down my face into my beard.

If I had died there, it would have been from joy,

the joy that you were coming to Provence,

to Arles, and to the yellow house to work with me.

Do you ever feel bliss when you're painting?

GAUGUIN

Sure, nothing gives me a fiercer erection

than a prone landscape or hills and gorges.

When I see a wet furrow hedged with bush

and sparkling with dew, I can't contain myself.

O the fucking landscape, oh, oh, oh!

[*Fakes masturbation.*]

Corporal, a hill is a hill, a bush is a bush.

[GAUGUIN *looks out of the window.*]

VINCENT

I know. I know Arles is not at its best now.
It's cold and dour and rainy in early winter,
the fields lost in fog, but come spring,
when lilacs foam from the hedges and spiky willows
hum their harp song in the wind,
you can't beat Arles in blossoming Provence;
the wheel ruts run into heaven and skylarks tumble
in the cerulean, not the slate-coloured, sky.
You'll see all that, we'll paint it together,
you'll forget the tropics, forget Martinique.

GAUGUIN

You know why you say that?

VINCENT

Tell me.

GAUGUIN

Because you come from a country
that's flat as this tabletop, boring as a sermon,
with a few desperate windmills to break things up.
So, naturally, when you came to Provence,
you were like a bum who discovers champagne,
but if you had ever seen gold-dripping palms
with their fronds muttering prayers to the azure blue
and the white crests of plunging breakers? Ah! Ah!
Compared to these pale flares of colour you call autumn . . .
I'm joking, Vincent. It is all very beautiful,

and I am deeply grateful to your brother.
Is that your favourite season then? Spring?

VINCENT

I love them all for different reasons. You?

GAUGUIN

I prefer countries that are seasonless,
with one light, all year, and without fog.
I think the future of art is in the tropics,
and no church, or not the one you worship.

VINCENT

I don't worship.

GAUGUIN

You're still a missionary.
With every stroke you do. It's a good thing.
I envy you your faith. No, I don't.
Look, the sun is making back with the earth,
little by little, stroke by cautious stroke,
like a lover's quarrel, but that square
of sunlight moving across the studio floor
is like a sail. You see, everything reminds me
of where I hope to be, eventually. Ah!
The sun in its full glory. Let's go out!

[*The room brightens.*]

VINCENT

That's the Peruvian, the pagan in you. Yes?

GAUGUIN

The barbarian, the hedonist! *C'est ça.* Let's go.
Soleil! Soleil!

[*He dances alone, then with* VINCENT.]

[LOTTE *stands in the doorway. She sees him dance.*]

VINCENT

This is the pure ecstasy of recognition!
You are the peasant beauty of my painting,
the same slate-coloured eyes, the orange skin.

GAUGUIN

That the Martinicans call *shabine.*

VINCENT

No, she is irrevocably Dutch.
I know my people, Gauguin.
What are you?

LOTTE

You can't see?

GAUGUIN

He means: Where're you from?

LOTTE

It doesn't matter.

VINCENT

Why are you here? In Arles?

LOTTE

Because of the Zouaves. The battalion.

VINCENT

You mean the soldiers?

LOTTE

The soldiers, yes, sir.
Most of my life is horizontal, sir.
They are my principal means of support.

VINCENT

Lotte, Lotte, just look at me. Turn round.
Don't you remember how in the Borinage
the miners sang their iron hymns at evening,
trudging home from work; the star-nosed mole
tunneled through the dirt and then the sky
was moving with miners' headlamps?
That was my province, yes;
you were the best part of it, Lotte.
You don't remember it? I painted you.
Not Provençal; slate-coloured countryside
and plodding windmills; you lit it up.

Say something to your old pastor in Dutch.
Do it. Speak Dutch to a homesick pilgrim.

LOTTE

What is all this? Sir, I can't speak Dutch.

VINCENT

Have you forgotten your own native tongue from living here?
It's happening to me. Remember it.

LOTTE

All right. *Voden für de wasser und der ciel.*

VINCENT

What is that?

LOTTE

It sounds like Dutch, no?
                    [*Laughs.*]
Und vest der longen.
                    [*Laughs.*]

VINCENT

I see. You think I'm crazy?

LOTTE

Don't touch me, please! You're frightening.

VINCENT

Who are you to say such things as
"*Noli me tangere*, for Caesar's I am"?
Don't touch me because I am Caesar's.
You're just a common whore.
       [*Bites her ear.* LOTTE *screams, clutches her ear.*]
Isn't that a sign of passion? Isn't it?

GAUGUIN

Hold on. I'll pour some oil on it. Wait, Vincent!

VINCENT

I'm sorry. Forgive me. I am so very, very sorry.

       [GAUGUIN *dabs at* LOTTE's *ear with turpentine on a rag.*]

LOTTE

Stop! You're putting paint in my hair!

GAUGUIN

Pardon.

LOTTE

It's he who should be asking for pardon!
Is it bleeding? Where's the mirror? Is it bleeding?

GAUGUIN

You're a fucking lunatic!

VINCENT

I know, I know.

LOTTE

You are both crazy and you both
have money for me. My fucking ear is bleeding!
You can't buy an ear just like that!
So you have to pay me something!

GAUGUIN

Pay her something, Vincent.

VINCENT

How much?

GAUGUIN

How much? I don't know how much.

VINCENT
[*To* LOTTE.]

How much?

LOTTE

I don't know how much. I never lost an ear before.

VINCENT

Ten francs.

LOTTE

Ten francs for a fucking ear!

VINCENT

How much, then? Paul, how much?

GAUGUIN

I don't know how much.

VINCENT
[*To* LOTTE.]

Ten francs and a painting.

LOTTE

Which one?

GAUGUIN

It's stopped bleeding.

LOTTE

It still fucking hurts.

VINCENT

This one.

[*Offers her a small painting of a drawbridge.*
LOTTE *examines it.*]

LOTTE

You see, if I had an ear, I could pull it so.

[*Pulls at the injured ear.*]

As if I were thinking. But I can't pull it.

It hurts when I try to pull it. Also

if you look hard, you'll see that the horse is crooked.

Give me something with big flowers on it. That one!

VINCENT

My sunflowers? Are you crazy? Not my sunflowers.

GAUGUIN

Give her back her ear and keep the sunflowers.

LOTTE

If I wasn't a whore, I'd call the police.

Give me the crooked horse and the fucking money.

GAUGUIN

Like an auction. Sold! Unwrapped. One crooked horse.

[*Gives the painting to* LOTTE.]

Scene Seven

[*A pile of lathes in a corner.* VINCENT *and* GAUGUIN,
measuring and hammering. Framing jute; sizing the canvases.]

VINCENT

So what now? We're abandoning canvas?
It's so coarse, jute. Heavy.

GAUGUIN

That's why I shipped so much down.
Jute is cheap; besides, it forces you
into another kind of brushstroke, heavier, thicker,
more impasto, blotting out that nervous
obsession with detail and dimensional shadow
you get with linen canvas, which costs a fortune.

VINCENT

It's wonderful to have you here, Paul.

GAUGUIN

We'll build a factory for the imagination.
The centre will shift from Paris to Arles.

[GAUGUIN *is cleaning up after* VINCENT.]

GAUGUIN

Look at this mess. Close your tubes.
Do you think being a genius means
you have to be untidy? To live in a pigsty?

VINCENT

No, Madame van Gogh. You're like a wife.

GAUGUIN

I don't swing that way. And I am also not your wife.

VINCENT

Well, all right. We'll just continue living in sin.

GAUGUIN

Sin! What is sin? What do you mean by sin?
You know, your brains have been beaten to a pulp
by Bible-thumping. Your thought is still
in bondage to the Borinage, among coal miners
and potato gobblers. You don't belong in Arles.
You have a northern soul, my friend.
Whores are meaningless. I mean real love.
You're a Protestant—you have a dutiful passion,
but you're incapable of sexual ecstasy.
I'm warning you: Don't let your solitude
corrupt our friendship. Or else
I'll be on the next screaming train to Paris.
You're not the first painter I've worked with!

VINCENT

My noble savage! My Peruvian!

GAUGUIN

I painted next to Pissarro and Cézanne.
Men! Neither of them made
those little queasy overtures of anything
more than professional friendship.

VINCENT

Did they support you? Like Theo?

GAUGUIN

I pay my way, Vincent. Don't insult me.

VINCENT

I'm going out. Are you coming?

[VINCENT *puts on his dark blue overcoat.*
GAUGUIN *is smoking his pipe.*]

GAUGUIN

Ho! You look like a Confederate general.

VINCENT

Well, we have our own little civil war here.
But you mean a Union general.
Blue was for the Union; Confederates wore grey.
As you may have noticed, my coat is blue.

GAUGUIN

You're such a bloody scholar, you know!

VINCENT

I know. I can't help it. I'm just being accurate.

GAUGUIN

You'd be a better painter if you were less accurate.
You lack imagination, Van Gogh. You're too accurate.

VINCENT

I see. Unlike you.

GAUGUIN

Did you hear me say that?

VINCENT

[*Pulling out canvases, showing them.*]
Accurate! You call these accurate?

GAUGUIN

Like Monsieur Meissonier. Accurate buttons.
Accurate leaves.

VINCENT

Red grass. Green sky. The Gauguin style.
Great imagination but totally inaccurate.

GAUGUIN

I pay my way, Vincent. Don't insult me.

VINCENT

No, you don't pay your way. My brother does.

GAUGUIN

I signed a contract with Theo. The one I keep
folded in my pocket day and night.
That I'd paint x number of canvases
for his gallery in Paris for the rent.
Besides, those men were greater company.
Pissarro and his cloudy beard. Cézanne.
Great friends, not whiners and complainers. Not Dutch . . .
[*Pause.*]
Why did you ask me here?

VINCENT

From solitude.

GAUGUIN

Solitude? What solitude?

VINCENT

From loneliness.

[*A dry sob.*]

GAUGUIN

Vincent, I love you. You know that.

[*Comes to* VINCENT *and puts an arm around
his shoulder. Embraces him.*]

4 5

VINCENT

I'm sorry.

GAUGUIN

Don't be. Tell me again.
Describe it to me again now. Vincent's dream.

VINCENT

Laval, who was with you in Martinique . . .

[*Fade.*]

Scene Eight

[*Heavy knocking.* GAUGUIN *goes downstairs to
open the front door.*]

GAUGUIN

Yes! Coming! This is like a railway station.

[*He opens the door. The* PROPRIETOR *brushes past*
GAUGUIN *to enter the studio, sees* LOTTE, *nods to her.
She nods in return. The* PROPRIETOR *looks at all
the paintings on display.* GAUGUIN *enters.*]

PROPRIETOR

This is like a museum. Goodness me.
You did all of this?

GAUGUIN

Yes. What's the trouble, Monsieur?

PROPRIETOR

The gun, the gun.
I sold the pistol. I mean, he bought the revolver.

GAUGUIN

He bought— You sold three guns. Who?·

PROPRIETOR

No, one gun. Your friend with the red beard,
you know.

GAUGUIN

Vincent?

PROPRIETOR

The crazy Dutchman, yes, he made me.
He said he needed a gun to shoot hares.

GAUGUIN

Wait, wait! To shoot who . . . ? Who's Harris?

PROPRIETOR

Hares, hares . . .

[*Mimes his fist with two fingers for rabbit's ears,
leaping near* L O T T E, *who backs away.*]

He says they molest him
out in the fields when he's painting, like today.

GAUGUIN

Nonsense. Vincent wouldn't kill anything.

LOTTE

Unless he's crazy about rabbit stew.

PROPRIETOR

You know how sometimes he'll sit in the café
silent as a gravestone, all his nerves simmering
like boiling coffee, his whole body clenched
and staring; this morning at breakfast, he sat
staring at his usual table, so I came up to him
and asked him what he wanted and he pointed
to the hunting pistol I had mounted on the wall,
then he took out a fistful of francs, then
he gripped my hand and dragged me to the counter
and kept pointing to the pistol. His eyes
were as wild as dragonflies, so I took it down,
opened the case as he commanded, then
gave him bullets that I fetched from the drawer,
and he stormed from the café to shoot some hares.
I want the pistol back. I shouldn't have sold it.
Please, I could be in trouble with the police.
I have to report the transaction. It's the law.

LOTTE

The law? I'm going. Goodbye, Monsieur Gauguin.

[*Picks up her hat and shawl.* GAUGUIN *blocks her way, takes her hat and shawl.*]

GAUGUIN

Don't go yet. Sorry.
I wish I could help. Don't go to Paris. Stay here.

[*From the stair.*]

PROPRIETOR

I could go out in the fields and find him.

GAUGUIN

Yes! Thrash the corn and startle the rooks
and shoot them one by one, except he has the gun.
Charge him too much for one absinthe and . . .

[GAUGUIN *grabs the* PROPRIETOR *by the lapels with his left hand, and with his right hand miming a pistol, shoots him in the head.* LOTTE *shrieks.*]

Pow.

PROPRIETOR

Your friend is crazy! Asylum material! Ask her!

LOTTE

Don't ask me anything; even if I knew,
I have the inviolable secrecy of a prostitute.

[*Crosses her heart as she moves towards
the door, stops.*]

PROPRIETOR

I have the money for the pistol back. Here.

[*Shows a fistful of francs.*]

LOTTE

I can hold it for him. No?

GAUGUIN

No!

PROPRIETOR
[*To* LOTTE.]

What are you doing here?
[*To* GAUGUIN.]

What's she doing here?

LOTTE

What am I doing here? I'm here on business.

PROPRIETOR

Yeah, I know what kind of business.

LOTTE

You're a nasty man.

PROPRIETOR

[*To* GAUGUIN.]

You hear me say anything?
I said something. Tell me.

GAUGUIN

He may want to keep the gun. It's his.

PROPRIETOR

His eyes. When his eyes grip you so,
it's like two hands holding you. You have to obey
when he says, "I want to buy it." What could I do?

LOTTE

You could have not sold it.

PROPRIETOR

You see you?

GAUGUIN

I'll get the gun back.

[VINCENT *stands there, still carrying his easel,*
holding his new canvas of a cornfield. They all watch him.
He enters, removes his hat, puts the canvas down, then reaches

into the pocket of his blue greatcoat. He is standing in
front of the PROPRIETOR.]

PROPRIETOR

Don't shoot, don't shoot!
[LOTTE *is cowering against a wall.*]
Don't shoot, Monsieur.

[VINCENT *extracts a clay pipe from his pocket.*]

VINCENT

The wind. I would like to paint the wind;
when it draws a hectic shadow over the cornfields
it tunnels, churning all the olive groves silver, and
bending the pliant poplars, or it fans the stars
like candles and the constellations writhe and go out.
Yes. That, yes. Definitely that. Definitely.

GAUGUIN

Where's the pistol?

VINCENT

What pistol?

GAUGUIN

The one you bought.

[*Silence.* VINCENT *stuffs and lights his pipe. Grins.*]

VINCENT
The pistol is hidden. It remains my secret.

[*He sits in his armchair. Silence. Then he laughs.*]

[*Fade.*]

ACT II

Scene One

[*The studio.* VINCENT, GAUGUIN, THEO.]

VINCENT

How did you sleep, brother?

THEO

Angelically.

VINCENT

Really?

THEO

Yes. Apart from the train in the next room.

VINCENT

Train? What train?

THEO

[*Snores. Points to* VINCENT.]
That train. I forgot how you snored.

VINCENT

Me? Snore?

THEO

[*Punching him.*]
Coming to Provence was pure confirmation

of everything you gentlemen have painted.
The country went by in successive frames
in the train windows, like an exhibition.
Looking across the fields at some bruise-coloured clouds,
At some paralysed windmills and the rook-threshing dusk,
I thought, People will see this as a Van Gogh canvas;
so often great painters sign their names on landscapes,
making them immortal. Believe me,
you will make Arles immortal, Vincent.
And you, too, Paul.

GAUGUIN
Thank you, Monsieur.

[THEO *holds up a portrait.*]

THEO
For instance, who is this?

VINCENT
Our postman, Roulin.

THEO
A postman? With such a luxuriant beard?
Homeric! Vincent, you make the ordinary mythological.
And now, boys and girls, or just boys! Also,
ladies and gentlemen, or just, if I can call you riff-raff, so,
gentlemen, the financial report! Gather round, Messieurs.
Alors! Let this baguette represent Goupil's,

the gallery where I work. This bread knife is
the agent's cut, the bread loaf the poor artist,
namely, Gauguin. Normally I might have cut
the poor painter this pathetic slice about here,
and the sad wretch would have clutched his wheaten pittance
and gone home looking like something by Daumier—

                              VINCENT
or Millet—

                              THEO
              or Millet with his impecunious slice
of baguette.
But kindly notice how I edge the knife
nearer the middle of the loaf, and that, Messieurs,
is what has happened increasingly at Goupil's
to Monsieur Gauguin's output. Thousands of francs;
a growing popularity, including the purchase
of one painting by none other than Monsieur Degas,
who went into raptures over your work, Paul.

                              GAUGUIN
Degas bought one of my things?

                              THEO
Vincent, your work is taking time.
Be patient, brother. I bought one.

VINCENT

To be expećted. His work is prettier.

GAUGUIN

Pretty?

VINCENT

More decorative, I mean.

GAUGUIN

Well, fuck me!

VINCENT

Emblematic is what I mean.

GAUGUIN

Well, double fuck me! Anything else?

VINCENT

They buy him without understanding him.

THEO

Does that include me? I collect Gauguins.

VINCENT

You're a dealer, Theo. That doesn't mean
you know anything about painting.
I mean its spiritual procedure.

THEO

Oh, really?

[*Silence.* GAUGUIN *collects his money.*]

VINCENT

You expect me to be jealous, right? No?
You should know me better than that.
I am happy for you. I am happy without envy.

THEO

There's no need for that, Vincent.

VINCENT

Yes, there is. There is need.
You can see it in his face, that
pseudo-melancholy with which he draws
compassion for his miserable condition.
Poor Paul! With that smile—you see it?
That smile that says, "I'm patient.
I'm a genius, but I can wait my turn."
Well, his turn has come now, hasn't it?
A turn brought by our dear brother the art dealer.

THEO

Vincent, one day you'll sell. You'll see.

VINCENT

That's not the bloody point, you dolt!
You call yourself a dealer. You should
perhaps be selling kitchenware . . .

THEO

"Dolt" is not very nice, Vincent.

VINCENT

[To GAUGUIN.]

Say something. Don't just sit there like a bloody carving.

GAUGUIN

[Shrugs.]

What do you want me to say? I'm just good.
It took some time to be recognized,
but it will happen to you.

VINCENT

[Grinding his teeth.]

That is not the point.

GAUGUIN

Then what is the point, Vincent?

VINCENT

Not at all.

You talk about painting buttons, uniforms,
you jeer at Meissonier, but you're no different.

All of us want to sell our life's bloody work,
at the best prices, too . . . like Meissonier.

GAUGUIN

Sure, but—

VINCENT

No bloody "but"s . . .
We do.·

GAUGUIN

But we don't whore to do it, do we?

VINCENT

Don't we? Isn't that what we wanted? To sell
and to suddenly sell well. It changes men;
it changes style. The shadow of wealth
stalks all of us. Then it becomes the shadow of greed.

GAUGUIN

Corporal, I have lived all my life in the shadow
of the imp that dances on the point of a paintbrush: greed.
I am not hypocritical or pious. I am a venal whore.

VINCENT

Like Lotte.

GAUGUIN

No, not like Lotte; like me.
My name is Paul, the Peruvian prostitute.

VINCENT

You forgot one *P*—a painter. And a great one.

GAUGUIN

Thank you.

VINCENT

Come here.
Let me embrace you.
                    [*Hugs* GAUGUIN.]
Congratulations.

[THEO *hugs them both.*]

GAUGUIN

A little more, and then . . . Martinique.

VINCENT

You'll need a lot more than what you've made.

GAUGUIN

Perhaps two thousand francs in all.

THEO

Closer to four thousand francs, Paul.

GAUGUIN

Nah. Two.

VINCENT

Four thousand.
Besides, the more it costs, the longer you stay here.

THEO

Ah, Vincent, Vincent, Vincent . . .

GAUGUIN

Vincent. Just the width of his compassion makes him great.
He felt sad for the apples he painted, he commiserated
with uprooted onions, he raged
for the dying sunflower—that is what
other painters will say of this great man,
your brother. I have seen it myself.

[VINCENT *gesticulating.*]

THEO

What's he doing now?

GAUGUIN

He's preparing
for a larger version of *The Sower.*
He's just articulating the action,
the stride down the furrows, the flying seed.
It must seem crazy to the passerby.

THEO

You sure?

GAUGUIN

Except . . .

THEO

Except what?

GAUGUIN

He's crazy, Theo.

THEO

I know.
May the God I don't believe in help him.

[VINCENT *does some vehement
gestures as the Sower.*]

THEO

Were those for *The Sower*? These gestures?

VINCENT
[*Ignores the question.*]

You see this knee?

[*He rolls up a trouser leg.*]

This knee I placed
in the precise exact indentation, however faint,
of Our Savior's genuflexion in the legend.
It fit the echo of that imprint for which
Arles is legendary. Does that make me Our Savior?

GAUGUIN

No, that is one knee. Our Savior knelt with two.

VINCENT

Are you calling me a liar, Paul?

GAUGUIN

Me? No, no . . .

VINCENT

You believe me, Theo?

T·HEO

Whatever you say, Vincent.

VINCENT

No, not "whatever I say." "Whatever I say"
means you're humouring me. Are you?
Are you humouring this fool, this idiot, this liar
who is your brother?

[VINCENT *confronts* GAUGUIN.]

And who may you be?

[*They face each other.*]

GAUGUIN

[*After a while.*]

I'm Paul.

VINCENT

The apostle?

GAUGUIN

[*Smiling slowly.*]

The painter.

VINCENT

Do I know you?

GAUGUIN

Yes.

VINCENT

Yes. There you were,
galloping on the road to—where was it again?—
when your name was Saul and you were suddenly
unhorsed by a lance of lightning. There's
a great painting of the event by Caravaggio, right?

GAUGUIN

Right.

[VINCENT *embraces him.*]

VINCENT

I'm in the middle. You're the two thieves.

[*Sinks to his knees, arms extended.*]

GAUGUIN

Yes.

[VINCENT *straightens up.*]

THEO

No, Paul.

[GAUGUIN *grabs* VINCENT *by the collar
and shakes him.*]

GAUGUIN

Yes, he is humouring you.
Because the sooner you confess
to your mental imbalance, Vincent,
the better for us all.

[*He releases* VINCENT.]

VINCENT

"He came unto His own, and His own received Him not." You
want to talk to my knee?

[GAUGUIN *gestures helplessly. He throws his arms
into the air and sits on a chair. He takes out his
pipe but does not light it.*]

GAUGUIN

No, thank you.

[VINCENT *crosses over to* GAUGUIN.]

VINCENT

Who are you?

GAUGUIN

Paul. You know me.

VINCENT

Paul the apostle?

GAUGUIN

Paul the painter. And you?

Who are you?

VINCENT

Rembrandt van Rijn.

GAUGUIN

[Nods, brows lifted encouragingly.]

VINCENT

Honoré Daumier.

[Shakes his head no.]

François Millet!

[Shakes his head no.]

No. I am Vincent van Gogh.

And I am very, very tired.

[Sobs, gropes for GAUGUIN.]

GAUGUIN

You are Vincent van Gogh, and I love you.

Theo, here's my estimate.

[Gives THEO a piece of paper, which VINCENT seizes, reads.]

VINCENT

Five thousand francs for Martinique. That estimate
would mean staying in Arles another year.

GAUGUIN

I'm not staying in Arles another year.

No way am I staying here another year.

Two thousand francs'll be enough.

[GAUGUIN *embraces* VINCENT *fiercely.* THEO
comes over and all three embrace, sobbing.]

[*Fade.*]

[*Loud cawing. Deafening. Lights up as the three men break apart
and pack their things.* THEO *takes* VINCENT *'s hand in his.*]

THEO

Crows flew up suddenly as from a shotgun
when we broke from our embrace. Sunset raged
with apocalyptic fury over the cornfield
to the cacophonous harmony of the crows
as I took my brother's hand and we walked home
followed by the pipe-puffing melancholy Frenchman.

[*Fade.*]

Scene Two

THEO

I'm getting married, Vincent.

VINCENT

You wrote me that.
At least you indicated it. Same woman?

THEO
[Laughing.]
Of course.

VINCENT
So I'm not surprised. Maybe
a little disappointed, but not surprised.

THEO
You don't want me to get married? Disappointed?

VINCENT
For very selfish reasons. Obviously.
With a wife, who'll take care of me? Of us?

THEO
[In fake astonishment.]
You're two big men! You aren't little boys.
In addition to seeing how you both live,
I wanted to bring you the news myself.

VINCENT
I appreciate that, but it's not really news.
[Pause.]
As I said.
[Silence.]

THEO

Vincent, I feel,
I feel a sort of sullenness building up.
I need someone to look after me, too.
By the way, where's the pistol?

VINCENT

Oh, no!
Not that one. "Where's the pistol?" The pistol is safe.
You thought you'd catch me off guard
about your marriage, then shoot the question.
"Shoot the question." That's pretty good. So?

[*Long silence.*]

THEO

Why don't you get married?

VINCENT

To whom?
You know any woman who would have me?

THEO

Anybody. Even to that girl who comes
in and out of the house! No, seriously.
I want you to wish me luck and happiness, Vincent.

VINCENT

Both? Luck and happiness? Why not?
I've never been lucky or happy with women.

THEO

Someday it will happen.

VINCENT

Like selling my work.
Why don't I sell my goddamned paintings, Theo?

THEO

Because they are crude, in the way Giotto
and Masaccio are crude.

VINCENT

Try and sell them.

THEO

Jesus Christ, I can't believe you said that!
What the fuck do you think I've been doing?

[GAUGUIN *appears*.]

GAUGUIN

You gentlemen all right?

THEO

Are we disturbing you?

VINCENT

Disturbing him? It's your house. You pay for it.

[GAUGUIN *lets that pass.*]

GAUGUIN

I'm going to the café. Shall we have lunch?
I'm paying with Monsieur van Gogh's money.

THEO

No lunch. I'm leaving very shortly.
I'll say goodbye now, Gauguin. *Au 'voir.*

GAUGUIN

Thank you enormously. For everything.
Can I help with your luggage to the station?

THEO

No, thanks. I'm fine. Shall I give Degas
your regards?

GAUGUIN

Degas. Him only,
not those other prostitutes. *Merci encore.*

[GAUGUIN *gets his coat and beret, dresses.*
More silence. Then GAUGUIN *exits.*]

THEO

Do you know what I believe in, Vincent?

[*He is packing as he talks.*]

I believe in what you're doing now
and also what you have done. I look at some church
that you have painted, and to ordinary eyes
it's crooked, tilted, awkwardly drawn,
even warped, but you paint with phenomenal conviction
what that church means to you, not its architecture
but its faith. You paint an olive tree and it becomes
a parable in paint, a cypress is a leaping flame
that doesn't singe, your strokes, your paintings,
have a biblical authority, your visual language—
all this has made me proud, and immensely grateful
to be your brother. Goodbye, my dear brother.
Yes, weep. I am weeping, too. It's love, Vincent.
It's only love. It is our privilege. *Adieu.*

[*They embrace.*]

It's worked out pretty well, hasn't it?

VINCENT

What?

THEO

The arrangement with you and Paul.

VINCENT

You think so?

THEO

Yes, one of the best things
I've ever done in my life.

VINCENT

I won't see you again.

THEO

Don't say that.

VINCENT

I know it.

THEO

Nonsense.

VINCENT

You are more than a brother.
I know and will never know anyone
who embodies such charity.

THEO

I'm going.

I'll see you soon.

[VINCENT *shakes his head no.*]

THEO

If you can't come to my wedding, I'll understand.

[*Silence.*]

You both produced such tremendous work
of such consistent beauty.

VINCENT

Thanks to you.

THEO

Goodbye, Vincent. *Ave atque vale,*
as Catullus said. Bye, brother.

VINCENT

Theo.

[*They embrace.*]

[*Fade.*]

Scene Three

[The studio. LOTTE *knocks.*
GAUGUIN *opens the door.]*

GAUGUIN

Lotte? It's you! Come in, come in.

[She enters. Removes hat, shawl.]

LOTTE

Hello, Monsieur Gauguin.

GAUGUIN

Where have you been?
Have you left Arles?

LOTTE

I went to Marseilles.
It didn't quite work out. These are nice.

GAUGUIN

Memories of Martinique. Vincent's out painting.

LOTTE

I saw him go out. I was in the café. I knew that.

GAUGUIN

He's in a frenzy of production.

LOTTE

Is he better?

[*She touches one temple.*]

GAUGUIN
[*Shrugs.*]

What's "better"? He's a good man, you know.

LOTTE

Oh, I know that. All you artists are a little crazy.
Can I sit somewhere?

GAUGUIN

Sure. Sorry.

[*Silence.*]
[*He clears a stool. She sits. Silence.*]

Lotte, I won't flatter you. You look like hell.

[*Silence.*]

LOTTE

That's because I'm dying, Monsieur Gauguin.

GAUGUIN

Dying? Nonsense. Dying of what?

LOTTE

Of tradition. Like the novels, the theatre.
Of the prostitute's complaint; you know.

GAUGUIN

Then that's wonderful. It's set your cheeks ablaze.
Your eyes are shadowy but piercing. The disease
has grown you a tragic grandeur, a definition.
A fate.

LOTTE

Oh, thank you. Fate? Just for me?
Does it also entitle me to a little cognac?

GAUGUIN

Oh, certainly! Certainly! What a pig I am!
Is that what Marseilles did to you?

LOTTE

It took all the little money I had left.
It's a disgusting, ravenous city. Do you know it?

GAUGUIN

Every sailor knows Marseilles.

LOTTE

Did you like it?

GAUGUIN

It's more honest than Paris.

LOTTE

You really think so? You believe that?
Yes, Marseilles is the country of fog. It is the replica
of my soul, Marseilles. It was there I found
that I had one. That everybody has one, of course.
But when everything begins to lose its name, as if
God had taken a big eraser and was rubbing out
everything that had a name, and that after a while
your turn was coming, that a street was coming
and even a lamp that was rubbing out and rubbing out
and then you couldn't see your arm in front of you
or the next house, and as if suddenly there
was no alphabet and nothing to correspond,
no adjective, no echo, just grey stone
that melted in you and folded back again . . .
I lost my flesh in the fog, I lost my name,
and any reason for being; it was like the steam
in a railway station, but the train had gone
and left me on the platform alone, then nothing
but the smoke that vanished from this miserable life.
That is Marseilles to me, a fading fog. M'sieur,
my life was distributed in pieces by the fog.
I haven't quite collected the pieces yet.
I have read so many ceilings
from lying on my back.
What are you reading?

GAUGUIN

Zola.

LOTTE

I have never read him. I don't read much.

GAUGUIN

And I could have made a fortune in the stock market.
Arles is another name for emptiness.
How could the afternoon be so empty?
It is empty because of its fullness.
Because of the silent sorrow of the twisted olives,
because of the anguish of the pointed cypress,
because of the hot silence of that madman's head.

LOTTE

Are you married?

GAUGUIN

Married, yes.
I was married, but I needed freedom.

LOTTE

Poor woman.

[GAUGUIN *starts painting. Scraping a canvas onto a mat.*]

GAUGUIN

Poor Mette. Very true.

I sank into a depth of mental squalor

after our separation. Drink, compulsive whoring.

A savage self-contempt about my work.

My hands trembling with the tremor of suicide.

One morning I watched her cradling a cat

and I knew that I would love her to this day.

LOTTE

Did all the women there run around naked?

In Martinique, I mean.

GAUGUIN

No, no. You see, the eye of the nipple kept staring back

at the missionary, her sex kept its lips shut.

She was like an orange lily sheathed in chastity,

so he wrapped her in a floral winding sheet,

and civilization as we know it was saved.

That sheathing of her cinnamon-hued skin

saved us from typhus, dysentery, cholera,

from civil discontent and war. Yes! Just one sheet.

Purity's panacea, do you understand?

LOTTE

No, sir.

GAUGUIN

Nor did they, but they wore it. Wear.

LOTTE

Comprends pas. I don't follow.

GAUGUIN

I am talking about the tropics as
not merely a religion of the sun
as the shipping agencies would have it; no,
as something deeper, something more profound;
all those disfigured faces on the train
are dreaming of a life beyond their own
constricted train tracks. Their private Martiniques,
not Paris, either; Paris is not Paradise.
Paris n'est pas Paradis.
No matter what they tell you.
[*Pause.*]
All those fierce horizons! Always receding.

LOTTE

Is that the port from which you went to Martinique?

[*Silence. She gets up and walks around.*]

GAUGUIN

Yes. You know, we are doing quite well.
Not Vincent so much, but yours truly, quite well.

LOTTE

Send me to Paris, please, Monsieur Gauguin?
My breasts are unaffected; they are still firm towers.

One day they may topple, but not quite yet.
Are there such towers in Paris? I'm sure there are,
but they come with intelligent conversation
and their familiarity with art.

GAUGUIN

You're already wearing Parisian colours;
your dress is the smoky black of an iron express,
your bonnet and your cheeks are an orange fire.
You're there already, you don't need me.

Wait! Hold on! Let me show you something.
                    [*He brings her a drawing.*]
I found my self-portrait: a head by Masaccio in 1425.
From *The Tribute Money*, brown hair, alert eyes,
hazel, a light brown beard. Isn't it me? Amazing!
I've been immortal all this while! The power of painting.
Isn't this me? Isn't it remarkable?
This prophecy?

LOTTE

Yes. It's you.

GAUGUIN

I always knew I was immortal, Lotte.
Look there, sweetheart, and you'll behold
an ineradicable nobility of feature.
My girl, you have been consorting with a prince
of the Peruvian royal family. *Regarde!*

[Shows his profile.]

LOTTE

Can the prince send me to Paris? Please.
I'll pay him back.
Your Highness.

GAUGUIN

Pay me back?
How many Zouave soldiers will that take?

LOTTE

Let me die in Paris with smoke passing the windows
and flags flying from the chimneys and the swallows
twittering my requiem, and the bats like acolytes
saying goodbye to a sobbing concertina
from an economical café. That's what I wanted
always on my tombstone. Help me, *monsieur le prince.*
My family's from there, you know.

GAUGUIN

Is that so? Listen. You know who I am?
I am Gérard de Nerval's prince.
                    [Recites.]
Je suis le ténébreux—le Veuf—l'inconsolé,
Le Prince d'Aquitaine à la tour abolie:
Ma seule étoile est morte, et mon luth constellé
Porte le soleil noir de la Mélancolie.

I am the dark one, the widowed, the inconsolable,
the prince of Aquitaine in the demolished tower;
my only star is dead; and my lute's fable
brings the sun's black, melancholy flower.
This is my poem to Martinique:

> [GAUGUIN *searches among the paints, finds it.*]
> *The coconut fronds talk to one another.*
> *I try to understand their agitated conversation.*
> *I learn only this: that they do not care whose*
> *reputation increases on the Rue de Commerce,*
> *who paid for lunch today in the Café Royale,*
> *for the satieties of the Salon. The mongoose*
> *that burrows under a pile of palm branches*
> *so easy to catch fire is not concerned today,*
> *despite his sniffing and enquiring nose,*
> *with the deals of the galleries. The palms*
> *give me that lesson in their magnificent tossing—*
> les palmiers, les cocotiers *with their triumphant plumes,*
> *that blue which has taught me a supreme indifference.*

> [GAUGUIN *smears blue paint on* LOTTE'*s face.*]
Now you are my little savage.

Scene Four

[VINCENT *and* GAUGUIN. GAUGUIN'*s studio.*]

VINCENT

Are you leaving Arles?

GAUGUIN

Yes. No. I don't know.

[VINCENT *hands him a newspaper cutting.*
GAUGUIN *reads it.*]

"The murderer took flight"?
Is this me? Am I "the murderer"?

VINCENT

Aren't you taking flight
by returning to Paris?

GAUGUIN

Returning to Paris is not the same thing
as not going to Martinique.

VINCENT

I see. What's this, Peruvian logic?

GAUGUIN

"Murderer." Whom have I killed?

VINCENT

There are various kinds of death, my dear friend.

GAUGUIN

Corporal, you're right. Anything for peace.

Scene Five

[*Early night. A street near the house. Two street lamps.*
GAUGUIN *walking home with a bag of groceries. He hears steps
behind him. When he walks, the steps grow closer. He stops. The
steps stop. He quickens his pace. So do the steps. He is now in an
arc of light from a street lamp. He stays out of the light and hides
against a wall, waits.* VINCENT, *holding an unsheathed razor,
comes into the light. He looks around wildly, then freezes as*
GAUGUIN *comes into the light.* VINCENT *and* GAUGUIN
stare at each other a long time, VINCENT *holding the razor
threateningly.* GAUGUIN *walks slowly up to* VINCENT,
*who now looks amazed that he is holding a razor. He backs
away from* GAUGUIN, *then turns and plunges into the
outer dark.* GAUGUIN *continues on his way home.*]

[*Fade.*]

Scene Six

[VINCENT *is trying on a hat whose rim holds lit candlesticks.*]

GAUGUIN

Vincent, what the fuck are you doing?

VINCENT

I'm trying to realize perception.

GAUGUIN

What is perception? Those little chunks of light
through which we glimpse the infinite?
Bad carpentry. The sum of all our knowledge.

VINCENT

Plus none of us has really painted the stars.
The only way to paint them is by starlight,
not the bright flecks in some shuttered studio—
their stars are decorations without energy.
I will be the first painter to paint the night,
the night as it really is: a pit, a tunnel, a sewer,
a painting you can fall into like a chasm
with all the terror of infinity.

GAUGUIN

Vincent, you're going to burn the damn house down.

VINCENT

Oh, what are you so afraid of, Paul?

GAUGUIN

Fire. Do you think I came here for
the thrill of the sun? For weather? For moonlight
or starlight? For the climate? I came for
a word you use too often—for my soul. To find
some explanation for my pain, some
simple explication of my unshakeable curse,
which a thousand candles cannot illumine,

and that explication is not in faith
or in madness, but maybe in Art. Go on, burn the damn house.

[Exit.]

[V I N C E N T *appears on a hilltop overlooking Arles; lamps,
stars, streets ablaze.*]

VINCENT

O starry, starry night, how shall I exult?
Your fruit hangs heavily in the black sky,
your floor is scattered with the fallen crystals
of the remembered constellations, your orbs plummet,
your lucid fountains jet surpassing praise,
your tears, the gliding sorrow of some behemoth,
are like a thousand pharoses on the dark sea;
processional pilgrims and sentinels
over our streets and cities, steer us home.
Home, home to heaven. O starry, starry night!

[Fade.]

Scene Seven

[*Flags, crowd noise, fireworks, and approaching martial music.
Early afternoon. The café front decked out. The* P R O P R I E T O R
*wearing a large municipal ribbon and a top hat enters and
mounts a chair, a speech in his hand.* V I N C E N T, G A U G U I N,
and L O T T E *enter.* G A U G U I N *hoists* L O T T E *onto a chair*

9 3

to better see the parade. Y O U N G   R O U L I N, a Zouave, is in
the street marching. The crowd roaring.]

PROPRIETOR

Not only as a proprietor but as deputy mayor,
I have written this encomium to the empire.
[*Shouts.*]
Cayenne, Algérie, Maroc, Martinique,
wherever the fleur-de-lis shall flourish
in our devoted colonies, and our culture take root,
irradiate from Provence to Burgundy,
for here in inconsequential Arles, we, too,
contribute to the flowering of France
by love, by sacrifice, by military service;
among these noble warriors is one
of the humble issue of Monsieur Roulin,
a postman, a fine, upstanding issue
of a patriot wearing different, perhaps
a little more elaborate and ornate garb
than the blue tunic and brass buttons of his father,
but also in uniform. That of a Zouave.
[*Louder applause.*]
Both sons of France, both citizens of Arles,
both sharers of one vision: triumphant France
giving her arts and glory to the world,
bringing her radiance to barbaric tribes,
to docile colonies, in the Republic's name.
Cayenne, Algérie, Maroc, Martinique.

Hooray for grenadier and corporal.
The Zouave Roulin.

                    LOTTE
He's beautiful.
                    [*Shouts.*]
You are beautiful, Roulin.

                  VINCENT
             [*Shouts to* LOTTE.]
He's your meat. All yours.
Lambs to the slaughter, all of you!
Bloody lambs! Roulin the lamb!

                  GAUGUIN
Vincent! Show some respect!

                  VINCENT
Not lambs, pigs! Piglets! All of you!

                 PROPRIETOR
Have some respect, Monsieur!

                  GAUGUIN
                    It's okay, it's okay.
He's a Dutchman. They lost their empire.

                  VINCENT
I can strut, too, I can march, I can blow

reveille on a bugle. Where's my band?
I am a local patriot. Where's my parade?
                    [*Disgusted.*]
Ho! Piglets, follow me!
                    [*Marches.*]
They do not recognize artists, Corporal.

                    PROPRIETOR
You are making a scandal in front of my café.

                    VINCENT
You make a lovely figure, young Roulin.
You make a lovely rabbit for the stew
that the imperial powers make of you,
for the admiration of young boys and whores,
but not of artists. March on, march on
to fall into the grave's carnivorous jaws
for a bright rag. Let us go home, Corporal.
We fight a war harder than any of theirs.

[VINCENT *withdraws a pistol, waves it around laughing,*
then surrenders it to GAUGUIN.]

Scene Eight

[*Sidewalk.* LOTTE *and* YOUNG ROULIN.
The PROPRIETOR *takes their order.*]

PROPRIETOR

Deux fous alors. I know your father.
He delivers the mail excellently.

LOTTE

You're a fine young man
and I don't want to spoil your life.

YOUNG ROULIN

What if I want you to spoil it?

LOTTE

No.

[VINCENT *enters with a bandaged head, carrying*
a small box. He places it on the table.]

[*Sees* VINCENT.]

Hello, Monsieur van Gogh.

VINCENT

Hello, Lotte. I have a present for you.

YOUNG ROULIN

Alors, I shall see you again. *Non?*

LOTT.E

I don't think so. Go and find a lover.
Find a war. Not a whore.

[YOUNG ROULIN *exits.*]

[*To* VINCENT.]

What's all this paint on it?
My God, it's not paint. Is it blood?

VINCENT

It's the rest of your ear.

LOTTE

The rest of my ear?

VINCENT

The remainder. Yes. I owed you that.

[*She faints.* VINCENT *props her up. Takes out his pipe.
Smokes.* LOTTE *is propped up in her chair.*]

You're blest, you have known two great painters.
There were great differences in our techniques.
You see, Paul divided the canvas sectionally
and without shadows with a moral simplicity,
or rather, a severity that he denies.
We were both named for saints, Vincent and Paul.
Whoever called me Vincent may have thought of

some saint, of course, but I like to think of Vincent
as sunlight through a drizzle. Can you see it?
Vin. Vin is wine. Wine and the sun,
with that incredible light that a drizzle brings.
Vincent, whereas Paul now sometimes signs
his name to mean a prick *gros*, big prick, Gros Guin.
Despite my ambitions I have always been
afraid that I might produce a masterpiece—
then I might stop working. I love failure.
I love failure because it is the spur
that wakes you up the next day to work, to drive you,
to whip you like a damn mule to do better.
But always there's this terror of success.
Vincent is a drizzle blowing across the olives
and making them even silverer, if there's such a word.
Vincent is black crows rising from a cornfield. Oh!
I feel quite faint. I'm going home to rest now.

[*Exits, singing his hymn.*]

Scene Nine

[*The café.* LOTTE *sitting up. The* PROPRIETOR,
GAUGUIN.]

GAUGUIN
Of course they will ask! How could he do such a thing?

PROPRIETOR

What? Did he cut her throat? The madman!
I'm calling the police.

GAUGUIN

I want to stay here. One room.
Go for my things in his house.
[*Embraces* LOTTE.]
And when you get better,
we will go to Paris and then to Martinique.
The sea there. The beautiful sea.
The light! You hear me, Lotte?

LOTTE
[*Smiling.*]
Yes. We'll go there. Together. Martinique.

GAUGUIN

I promise you my love. Your Paradise.

[GAUGUIN *embraces her more tightly.*]

[*Fade.*]

Scene Ten

[PROPRIETOR *sweeping.* VINCENT *enters.*]

VINCENT

So he has not been here?

PROPRIETOR

No, we have not seen him.

VINCENT

His room is empty. But the bed is made,
white and pure as a snowdrift.
You're sure he didn't sleep in the hotel?

PROPRIETOR

You're a dangerous man.
Why shouldn't he keep away from you?

[VINCENT *goes to sit down.*]

Please don't sit down.

[VINCENT *gets up.*]

VINCENT

I understand.
I went down to the station, looking for him.
Just in case he took the train to Paris.
But he still has a few things in his room.

[*Silence.*]

He has gone to Martinique. I'm sure.

PROPRIETOR
Where?

VINCENT
Martinique.

PROPRIETOR
[*Cleaning a glass; holds it up to the light.*]
Where's that? Oh, Martinique!

VINCENT
The other side of the world.
A paradise on the other side of the world.
If you should see him . . .

PROPRIETOR
I'll tell him.

VINCENT
Tell him I still love him.
I will always love him.

PROPRIETOR
That kind of message
you should give him yourself.
Please now move along, sir.
People are watching.

VINCENT

I understand.

Please tell him the corporal loved him.

The corporal wanted to tell him goodbye.

[VINCENT *exits, singing his hymn.*]

[*Fade.*]

Epilogue

[T H E O, *in Paris, reading a letter.* G A U G U I N
walking alone in Paris.]

GAUGUIN

This is your favourite rascal. Paul. In Paris.

Dear Theo. I went for a last walk along

Les Alyscamps, without saying goodbye

to the thin, consumptive poplars, to the things

I had grown along with for months.

The bald benign owner who had first befriended

me was not sweeping in front of the door to his café,

but he would be there tomorrow. I would not.

[*We see the* P R O P R I E T O R *sweeping, then stopping.*]

I have never heard of a whore who ended well.

I think Lotte is dead; either that or she

has paid for her own steerage to Martinique.

I don't know. She hasn't written. I have not seen her.

I am leaving Vincent. Ha! This would be more true

than loving, since he has worn me out. As for Lotte . . .

[*Two shots ring out. He pauses. He resumes.*]

The belief in paradise that I infected her with

was with her for life. In a way we all had it:

Vincent with his vision of an artists' settlement,

and mine, too, in Martinique. In this brown season,

when all the leaves are either withering or falling

with gestures of surrender similar to mine.

My desertion is natural. I have met no man

as compassionate as your brother, a saint,
says Saint Paul to Saint Vincent. Tell him nothing.
Except I loved him, but I had to go.

(Fade to black.)

END

Printed in the USA
CPSIA information can be obtained
at www.ICGtesting.com
LVHW091147150724
785511LV00005B/586